W9-AZD-281

WITHDRAWN

Great Explorers

Ferdinand Magellan

by Jim Olhoff

Visit us at www.abdopublishing.com

Published by ABDO Publishing Company, 8000 West 78th Street, Suite 310, Edina, MN 55439. Copyright ©2014 by Abdo Consulting Group, Inc. International copyrights reserved in all countries. No part of this book may be reproduced in any form without written permission from the publisher. ABDO & Daughters™ is a trademark and logo of ABDO Publishing Company.

Printed in the United States of America, North Mankato, Minnesota
052013
092013

Editor: John Hamilton
Graphic Design: Sue Hamilton
Cover Design: Neil Klinepier
Cover Photo: Alamy
Interior Photos & Illustrations: Alamy-pg 19; AP-pg 20; Corbis-pgs 15, 18, 24 & 29; Getty-pgs 9, 12-13, 15, 16-17, 21 & 26-27; Granger Collection-pgs 5, 22-23, & 25; iStockphoto-compass illustration; John Hamilton-pg 11 (map); Jose Malhoa, artist-pg 8; Peter Paul Rubens, artist-pg 11; Princeton University Library-pg 32; Thinkstock-pgs 4, 6, 7, 10, 14 & grunge map background illustration.

ABDO Booklinks
To learn more about Great Explorers, visit ABDO Publishing Company online. Web sites about Great Explorers are featured on our Book Links pages. These links are routinely monitored and updated to provide the most current information available. Web site: www.abdopublishing.com

Library of Congress Control Number: 2013931667

Cataloging-in-Publication Data

Ollhoff, Jim.
 Ferdinand Magellan / Jim Ollhoff.
  p. cm. -- (Great explorers)
ISBN 978-1-61783-967-2
1. Magalhaes, Fernao de, d.1521--Travel--Juvenile literature. 2. Explorers--Portugal--Biography--Juvenile literature. 3. Voyages around the world--Juvenile literature. I. Title.
910/.92--dc23
[B]   2013931667

Contents

Magellan's World

Ferdinand Magellan was an explorer from Portugal who lived during the late 1400s and early 1500s. While commanding an expedition for Spain's King Charles I, he searched for a westward sea route to Asia. His expedition became the first to travel all the way around the Earth.

During Magellan's lifetime, Europe went through many changes. Sailors traveled farther on ocean voyages, and found new lands. New universities helped people learn about the world. Countries formed huge armies for their own protection—and to wage war on others.

During this time, Spain and Portugal had a very uneasy peace. They were jealous of each other's explorations and naval achievements. Sometimes the tension between them erupted into fighting.

Ferdinand Magellan, while searching for a westward sea route to Asia, led the first expedition to travel all the way around the Earth.

5

Cardamom

Star Anise

Nutmeg

Cinnamon

Cloves

Pepper

Above: Spices were valued greatly by Europeans of the 15th and 16th centuries. Getting these precious spices from Asia required a dangerous, often deadly, journey. But the spices were as valuable as gold.

Europeans desperately wanted to trade with Asian countries. Spices were of great value in Europe. Exotic spices like cinnamon, cloves, nutmeg, and pepper made food taste so much better. But spices wouldn't grow in Europe because the climate was too cold and dry. Spices grew in many parts of Asia, but Europeans thought the best spices came from the Spice Islands, in what is today Indonesia. These islands produced spices that were as valuable as gold in Europe.

Getting these spices, however, was a problem. The overland route to Asia was very dangerous because of bandits and hostile armies. An ocean voyage meant traveling south around the tip of Africa, and then traveling eastward. This was a very long trip, which meant malnutrition, disease, pirates, and dangerous storms.

European scholars knew that the Earth was round, but they argued about its exact size. They knew they could sail west from Europe and eventually reach the Spice Islands, but they had no idea how far away it was. In 1492, an explorer named Christopher Columbus found a landmass between Europe and Asia. Was this landmass part of Asia? Was it a big island? Or was it a major continent? They didn't know.

They also didn't know what they would find if they sailed to the other side of this landmass. Would there be sea serpents? Would there be seas of boiling water? Mapmakers often drew mythological creatures or fantastic dangers on their maps.

Europeans were frustrated. They wanted spices from Asia, but couldn't figure out how to get there safely and inexpensively. Then along came Ferdinand Magellan.

Overland trade routes between Europe and Asia were long and dangerous.

Magellan: Birth and Early Years

Above: Queen Lenore de Viseu took in 10-year-old Ferdinand Magellan when both of his parents died. Magellan became a servant in the royal court.

Ferdinand Magellan was born in Portugal in 1480. He was probably born in the Sabrosa region, in northern Portugal. His parents were friends of Portugal's royal family. Magellan's parents died when he was 10. The queen of Portugal took him in and he became a servant in the royal court. He received an education and learned about Portuguese ocean explorations. Portugal's sailors were some of the best in the world.

Magellan went on his first ocean voyage in 1505. He spent several years in and around India, trying to establish a Portuguese presence in the region. While there, he learned about the Spice Islands. He also fought in many battles, and traveled from one trading post to another. He returned to Portugal about 1512.

Magellan was a very independent and headstrong person. On a trip to Morocco with the Portuguese military, he was accused of selling goods to unauthorized traders, and leaving his post without permission. Instead of apologizing, he complained to the king that he wasn't making enough money. The king dismissed Magellan and refused to hire him again.

Magellan was determined to make a name for himself. He stubbornly pestered the king of Portugal with an idea to reach the Spice Islands by sailing west. The king would not give Magellan any ships. Refusing to quit, Magellan left Portugal and traveled to Spain. He hoped to offer his services to the Spanish royalty.

Above: A replica of a Portuguese caravel. This small, maneuverable ship was used by 15th-17th century Portuguese ocean explorers.

Mission: The Spice Islands

Below: A modern view of some of the Maluku Islands in Indonesia. They were once called the "Spice Islands."

Magellan wanted to travel to the Spice Islands (today's Maluku Islands in Indonesia). Many spices grew there, including cloves, mace, nutmeg, and others. These spices were very valuable in Europe. Magellan knew that if he could find a quicker way to the islands, he could become a very wealthy man.

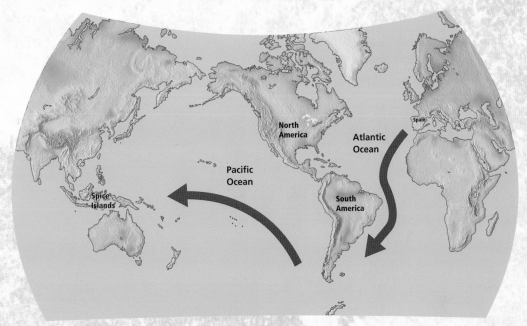

Above: Magellan's route to the Spice Islands involved traveling west from Spain. He planned to find a way around the large landmass, which we now know is North and South America.

Magellan had studied many maps and the voyages of Christopher Columbus. Magellan hoped to succeed where Columbus had failed: to get to Asia by sailing west from Europe. Magellan believed that he could get to the Spice Islands by traveling westward across the Atlantic Ocean. He knew there was a giant landmass in the way (what we know as North and South America), but he believed he could find a waterway through the obstacle.

Magellan visited Charles I, the king of Spain. King Charles wanted to open up trading ties with Asia. In 1518, he agreed to Magellan's plan, and gave the explorer the command of five ships.

King Charles I of Spain

The Voyage Begins

On September 20, 1519, Magellan and his five ships set sail from Spain. Magellan was on the flagship *Trinidad*, with a crew of 55. The biggest ship was the *San Antonio*, with a crew of 60. The *Concepción* had a crew of 45. The *Santiago* had a crew of 32, and the *Victoria* had a crew of 43.

The expedition's first stop was the Canary Islands, off the coast of Africa. These islands were controlled by Spain. They gave Magellan fresh supplies. After that, Magellan sailed to the southwest, heading for South America.

Magellan was careful to avoid Portuguese-controlled areas. The Portuguese were angry about the

Spanish voyage. Much of the eastern side of South America was controlled by Portugal. Magellan sailed south of these areas to avoid trouble.

On December 13, Magellan's ships anchored near today's Rio de Janeiro, Brazil. The crew obtained new supplies. Magellan believed that there would be a strait, a waterway, through South America to the Pacific Ocean. He sailed south along the eastern coast of South America, looking for this strait. On January 10, 1520, the expedition reached the inlet near modern day Buenos Aires, Argentina.

Below: King Charles I of Spain gave Magellan five ships. Magellan's goal was to find a fast way to get to Asia by sailing west from Europe.

Trouble on the Journey

The expedition continued traveling down the South American coast. In March 1520, Magellan was forced to create a temporary settlement to wait out the winter. He called the settlement Puerto San Julian, on the coast of today's country of Argentina.

Many of the sailors grumbled about the cold weather and frequent storms. Food was scarce. The crew began to lose faith in Magellan. They wondered if he was leading them to their doom. Many of the sailors were Spanish, and never trusted their Portuguese commander.

On April 1 and 2, three of the captains began a mutiny. They revolted against the leadership of Magellan. After a brief battle, the men loyal to Magellan defeated the mutineers. Magellan's quick temper took over, and he had some of the mutineers executed. Others he marooned on the shore of South America. Others were forgiven, and allowed to continue sailing with the expedition.

Above: In March 1520, Magellan's expedition faced cold, stormy weather as they traveled down the coast of South America. Their food supplies were low. Some sailors mutinied in April 1520. However, men loyal to Magellan defeated them. Magellan sentenced some mutineers to death. Others were marooned on South American shores. A few were forgiven.

Magellan had sent the *Santiago* farther down the coast to scout the area, but a sudden storm arose and the ship was wrecked. All of the crew made it to shore. Two men walked up the coast to tell Magellan what had happened. Magellan rescued the crew.

In October 1520, at the southern tip of South America, Magellan found a long waterway that he thought might be the path to the Pacific. He sent the *Concepción* and the *San Antonio* into the waterway to explore it. However, the men of the *San Antonio* disobeyed orders. They snuck out of the waterway and sailed eastward back across the Atlantic, heading home to Spain.

The waterway did lead to the Pacific Ocean, which was known as the South Sea at that time. The three remaining ships entered the strait. On November 28, 1520, they entered the Pacific Ocean. Today, that waterway is called the Strait of Magellan. The explorer named the ocean the *Pacific*, which means "still," because the water was so calm when they first entered it.

Death in the Philippines

Below: A statue of Lapu-Lapu, chief of the Mactan.

Once in the Pacific Ocean, Magellan's three ships sailed northwest. By March 1521, they had reached the Philippines. These are islands north of Indonesia and southeast of China. Magellan had an interpreter who could communicate with the people who lived on the islands. Magellan was able to make friends with some of the island peoples. One of the friendly leaders was Rajah Humabon, from the island of Cebu.

Rajah Humabon saw Magellan's advanced weaponry, and asked the explorer to help him fight his enemy on the island of Mactan. Magellan was anxious to befriend Rajah Humabon, thinking he might be of help later. Magellan agreed to fight Rajah Humabon's battle. Magellan's men advised him not to fight, but Magellan refused to listen. On April 27, 1521, Magellan led a small group of soldiers to the island of Mactan. Magellan's force was greatly outnumbered, and after a short battle, Magellan was killed. His body was never recovered.

Above: Magellan landed on the Philippine island of Mactan with a small group of soldiers. He intended to fight the local people in order to prove his friendship to the leader of another island. However, Lapu-Lapu, chief of the Mactan, brought all his forces. Greatly outnumbered, Magellan was killed by the Mactan on April 27, 1521.

The Voyage Continues

After the perilous voyage and the battle in the Philippines, less than half of Magellan's original sailors remained. They had three ships left, but not enough men to sail them all. They moved all the sailors to the *Trinidad* and the *Victoria* and then burned the *Concepción* so that no islanders could follow them. In May 1521, the two ships set sail, this time without their leader Magellan.

Local guides helped them navigate around the many islands, where reefs and shallow waters were treacherous. By November, they had finally reached the Spice Islands, fulfilling Magellan's original goal. The expedition traded with the local people and filled their ships with spices. They were now ready to continue their long westward journey back to Spain.

Below: A native village on the Spice Islands.

Above: A replica of the *Victoria,* one of Magellan's ships. In November 1521, the expedition's remaining two ships finally reached the Spice Islands. They traded with the native people and filled the *Victoria* and *Trinidad's* holds with spices.

Unfortunately, the *Trinidad* began to take on water. The sailors realized that the ship needed major repairs. They decided to split up. The crew of the *Victoria* would continue westward to Spain. The *Trinidad* would make repairs and then return eastward across the Pacific Ocean, going back to Spain the way they had come. After several weeks of repairs, the *Trinidad* began its Pacific Ocean journey, but was captured by Portuguese ships. It then sank in a storm while captive.

The *Victoria* sailed westward across the Indian Ocean. The ship's commander was Juan Sebastián Elcano. By May 1522, they were sailing around the southern tip of Africa. Supplies were running low. They were forced to ration their food. Many sailors starved.

Finally, on September 6, 1522, the *Victoria* arrived in Spain. Only 18 men were left from the approximately 250-member crew that started three years earlier. But Juan Elcano had brought Magellan's ship home, carrying cloves and cinnamon from the Spice Islands.

Juan Elcano and the 17 other surviving crewmen of Magellan's expedition arrived in Spain on September 6, 1522.

Juan Elcano: The First Real Circumnavigator

Below: The route of the first people to sail around the world. The journey started in 1519 with Magellan in command, but was completed by Juan Elcano in 1522.

Ferdinand Magellan usually gets credit for being the first to sail around the world. However, Magellan died halfway through the journey. In fact, Magellan didn't even intend to go around the world. He was simply trying to find a quicker and safer way to the Spice Islands.

Magellan's second-in-command, Juan Elcano, was the one who decided that the journey would continue after Magellan's death.

IL PRIMO VIAGGIO INTORNO AL MONDO 1519-1522

NORDAMERICA

OCEANO PACIFICO

EUROPA

ASIA

AFRICA

CINA CATIGARA

GIAPPONE

FILIPPINE

OCEANO INDIANO

SUDAMERICA

OCEANO ATLANTICO

AUSTRALIA

NUOVA ZELANDA

OCEANIA

JUAN FERNANDEZ

Left: Juan Elcano, Magellan's second-in-command, completed the around-the-world journey on September 6, 1522, returning to Spain with a hold filled with cloves and cinnamon from the Spice Islands.

It was Elcano who pushed through the Indian Ocean and around the southern tip of Africa. Elcano and the 17 other survivors of the expedition were the first people to sail all the way around, or circumnavigate, the globe.

Juan Elcano was born in the city of Getaria in northern Spain, in 1476. He was a sailor early in life, and signed on with Magellan in 1519. He was one of the men who started a mutiny in southern Argentina in April 1520. Magellan spared his life and forgave him.

After returning to Spain, Elcano became a hero. A few years later he went on another long voyage. Spain sent seven ships back to Asia. It wanted to establish a permanent settlement and a trading center. Elcano was one of the leaders of the expedition. Tragically, he died of malnutrition while sailing in the Pacific Ocean in 1526.

Magellan's Legacy

Opposite Page:
Magellan finds
the route to the
Pacific Ocean.
Below: Magellan
was an exacting
navigator. His
confidence and
determination
helped open the
world to trade.

Magellan's ship *Victoria* was the first to go around the world. Scholars already knew the Earth was round, but they argued about its exact size. Magellan's crew kept careful records of how far the expedition traveled. They were able to accurately calculate the size of the Earth.

The voyage also demonstrated the true nature of the oceans. It proved that the waterways of the Earth were all connected. Geographers of the time suspected that the landmass in-between Europe and Asia (what we know as North and South America) was not part of Asia. They thought it was a separate continent. The voyage of the *Victoria* gave geographers the proof they needed.

Magellan wanted to find a quick and easy route to the Spice Islands. While travelling westward from Europe was neither quick nor easy, it did open up travel and trade.

European countries immediately tried to establish trading centers in Asia. This brought good trade and commerce to some people in Asia. But it brought destruction to others, as overbearing European countries exploited the resources of rich Asian lands.

Despite this mixed legacy, Magellan and Elcano did what no one else had been able to do. They found their way around the world.

Timeline

1480	Ferdinand Magellan is born in Portugal.
1490	After the death of his parents, Magellan becomes a page in the royal court of Portugal.
1505	Magellan joins a Portuguese expedition to India.
1512	In Morocco, Magellan has a disagreement with a commanding military officer and leaves the service. He renounces his Portuguese nationality.
1518	Magellan convinces Spanish King Charles I to fund an expedition to the Spice Islands.
1519, Sept. 20	Magellan's expedition, with five ships and about 250 men, leaves Spain.
1520, April	Mutiny breaks out. Magellan regains control.
1520, November	Magellan's three remaining ships reach the Pacific Ocean.
1521, March	Magellan's ships reach the Philippine Islands.
1521, April 27	Magellan is killed in battle on the island of Mactan.
1521, November	The expedition finally reaches the Spice Islands.
1521, December	The *Victoria* continues westward under the command of Juan Elcano, heading home to Spain.
1522, Sept. 6	The *Victoria* reaches Spain. Only 18 men remain from the original crew.

A statue of Ferdinand Magellan in Punta Arenas, Chile, near the Strait of Magellan.

Glossary

CARAVEL

A small, fast ship used by Spanish and Portuguese sailors during the 1400s and 1500s.

CIRCUMNAVIGATE

To travel in one direction around the world, coming back to the starting point.

FLAGSHIP

The ship that the commander of a fleet sails on. Often the largest and most important ship in a fleet. Magellan started out his journey on his flagship, the *Trinidad*.

LAPU-LAPU

The leader of the Mactan. When Ferdinand Magellan tried to conquor the people of Mactan, Lapu-Lapu and his warriors killed Magellan and several of his men on April 27, 1521.

MACTAN

An island in the Philippines. Also, the native people living on that island.

MALNUTRITION

A poor diet consisting of either not enough food or not enough varieties of food. Sailors on long journeys often faced starvation or diets that did not have enough fruits or vegetables to maintain health. Some died of malnutrition.

MAROON

To purposely leave someone behind in an unknown place, often alone and without supplies needed for survival. Being marooned was a punishment for a sailor who has mutinied against their commanding officers.

MUTINY

When the crew of a ship disagrees with the captain and tries to forcibly take it over.

NAVIGATOR

The person in charge of plotting and directing the course of a ship.

PAGE

A servant in a royal court.

PIRATES

Outlaw seamen who capture and raid ships at sea to seize their cargo and other valuables.

SPICE ISLANDS

Islands in what is today Indonesia, famous for spices.

SPICES

Herbs and plants that flavor food. Common spices include cinnamon, mace, nutmeg, cloves, and pepper.

STRAIT

A narrow waterway that usually lies between two large land masses, connecting two bodies of water together. The Strait of Magellan lies between the Atlantic Ocean and the Pacific Ocean.

Index

Right: The *Victoria* was the first ship to sail around the world.